ONE DAY KNITTING MASTERY

The Complete Guide to Learn Knitting in Under One Day!

10 Step by Step Projects that Inspire you. Images Included

By Ellen Warren

Published by:

ALEX-PUBLISHING

Table of Contents

Note from Ellen Warren:

Welcome to the amazing world of knitting! As some of you know from my other books, this has been a passion of mine for more than 15 years, and I'm thrilled that you will allow me to help you learn this beautiful art form. Knitting has been a widely used skill all over the world since time immemorial. It is, basically, the method of turning thread or yarn into cloth by way of intermeshing it together. It can also be done by hand or by machine, but this book will mainly show you how to knit by hand. Learning this skill is very easy – by starting from the basics and progressing towards the more complex parts.

This book was made with the sole purpose of teaching you the basics of knitting. This book contains proven steps and strategies from a pro on how to begin knitting. You do not need prior training to read this book. Just read each step, have patience, and you will become a pro in no time.

Once you have read this book and complete the projects, you'll be well on your way to having both the skills and the confidence necessary to start trying your hand at a vast number of different knitting projects. Whether you want to sew for fun, help decorate your house, make yourself something new to wear, or hope to start a new business, you'll be surprised at just how fast you can pick up this new handicraft.

Knitting is a unique blend of art and manual skills. My roadmap is here to help you set off and learn how to craft a product to completion. Then, once you begin following a pattern, you may find that knitting is mainly a form of physical dexterity.

So whether you used to knit but fell out of the habit and are hoping to regain your lost skills, or you've never picked up hook and yarn, after reading this book you will be well on your way to creating dozens of beautiful, handmade items.

Let's get started!!

Ellen Warren

Chapter 1:
Choosing Your Knitting
Supplies and Tools

In learning this skill, choosing the right tools and supplies is essential to ensure amazing outputs. Making sure that you have the tools that you are more comfortable in using will help you learn – and put into practice your new skill – more quickly. Using tools that are smoothed for beginners is also essential, as using needles that are more suitable for people who are already experts may cause exasperation and difficulty on your part.

The use of quality tools and supplies is also essential, for only these will result in quality work output. You would not want to see your first output, after all your efforts, looking far from perfect due to the quality of materials used. Feeling the texture and thickness of the material will also benefit beginners who are not yet accustomed to this hobby.

Choosing Appropriate Wool/Yarn

A wise knitter will always consider the best wool or yarn to use in a chosen project. Choosing the appropriate type of yarn will significantly affect the outcome of the product. The chosen yarn or wool can also change the appearance, texture and quality of a project.

In choosing the yarn that you are going to use, take into account what kind of item you are creating. You have to consider if you want to make an item wearable, washable or just to keep you warm. These factors will affect your choice of wool or yarn, for each type of material can give different characteristics. Understanding that yarn, can be made from different types of material – silk, cotton, linen, cashmere, etcetera – is important, too, for considering the qualities you would like in your final product.

Things to Consider in Choosing Wool

• *Thickness*
  In choosing the thickness of the yarn that you

are using, it is easier for beginners to start off with thicker yarns. Thicker yarns are better for the beginner as it is easier to see the stitches and the loops you are making. A project will also be finished more quickly by using thicker yarns, which is beneficial for beginners – who can be encouraged by seeing a completed project within a reasonable timeframe.

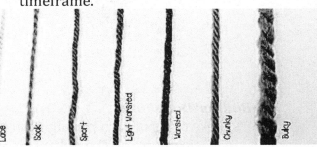

•Stretchiness

Choosing yarns that offer a little stretch will make maneuvering those complicated movements easier, especially for beginners who are still getting the hang of knitting.

Materials that are made from wool or animal fiber offer more stretch than other materials.

•Types of Yarn Bundle

A beginner might feel confused seeing the different kinds of bundles that yarn is packed in. Some may look gorgeous but are very hard to use when knitting.

▪Skein

By far, this type of yarn shape is the easiest to use. This is how most of the big yarn brands are wound, as it is the shape preferred by knitters. It is very easy to handle and you don't need to wind it again.

▪Balls or Doughnuts

These types of yarn packaging are also easy to knit from. The only problem with this type is that it may collapse towards the end.

▪Hanks

This may look like a very beautifully packed yarn, but knitting from one of these is very tricky. Yarn threads can wrap around each other if not handled properly. A technique that is used by some is to untwist a hank and put it in a circle, or wind it into a roll to make it easier to handle. It is a little time-consuming for beginners.

•Texture and Color

Choosing colors that are lighter are also much better for beginners. Avoid picking darker colors for now, even if you love those types, for it will make seeing the stitches harder. Settle with lighter colors first and start going for darker ones when you get the hang of it.

The texture of the chosen yarn is also paramount; choosing those that have smooth textures will help you see the stitches easier.

•Spun

Some yarns that are chained in a complicated way may cause problems for beginners because they are more prone to splitting. Choose simple spun yarns to help you avoid sticking your needle in the middle of the yarn.

In choosing the type of yarn or wool to start your project off, ensuring that you would love the effect of the selected material for your finished product is essential. Start with materials that are easier to handle so you can work faster and with ease; and then see a beautifully knit result from your new hobby.

Choosing Knitting Needles

Knitting needles are essential to the success of your project. Ensuring that you are using the appropriate needle for the yarn and the pattern you are making will have a significant effect on your finished product.

The needles also affect handling and working efficiency, especially for beginners who are still getting the feel of knitting. Using the wrong needle size will make working more difficult, especially when maneuvering hard stitches.

Knitting Needle Sizes

For beginners, the appropriate needle size specified by the pattern that you are using should be followed; but if you are not using a pattern, make sure that you are using a needle that is appropriate for the yarn size you are using.

Using needles that are thicker is also easier for beginners as they are more comfortable to grip and make learning easier.

Needle Numbers	Metric Measurement	Yarn Weight
0-1	1.5 mm-2 mm	Lace
1-3	2 mm-3.25 mm	Super Fine
3-5	3.25 mm-3.75 mm	Fine
5-7	3.75 mm-4.5 mm	Light
7-9	4.5 mm-5.5 mm	Medium
9-11	5.5 mm-8 mm	Bulky
13-19	9 mm-16mm	Super Bulky

Knitting Needle Shape

There are also a variety of needle shapes that are available on the market. The type of shape that is best depends on the knitter. Each person is different and what seems better for one person may not be good for another.

- •Straight Needles/Single-Pointed Knitting Needles
  This is the most commonly-known knitting needle shape; it is also best for making flat pieces. This type of needle is ideal for beginners as it is sharp or pointed at one end and has a cap on the other to hold the stitches in place.

•Double-pointed Needles

This type of needle has points on both end, and is used in knitting seamless, circular items. Beginners may have a hard time using this kind of needle as it does not have a cap on the end to keep the stitches in place.

•Circular Needles

These are two straight needles that are joined together in a flexible plastic cord that comes in different lengths. Used for a variety of projects, often for larger-sized items.

•Cable Needles

Needles that may be hooked or straight and come in very short lengths; are basically used in making knitting cable stitches.

Knitting Needle Material

Your skill level should be considered in choosing needle material for knitting, especially for beginners. Choice of material will hinder or improve your efficiency, and it is best to choose materials that are not slippery for it will not help you hold your yarn in place.

•Bamboo Needles

This is a splendid choice for beginners; they are not slippery and will hold your yarn in place. They are also very light and flexible, and are the best choice for people with arthritic hands. The only downside with this type of material is that it can bend and break.

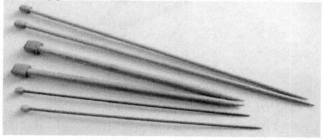

•Wooden Needles

Also a superb choice for beginners; it has a smooth texture but will not let yarn slip easily, which is especially useful when using slippery fibres. But, like bamboo needles, they also tend to easily break.

•Plastic Needles

This type is also very popular, especially for those who already know how to knit. These are very light and flexible and do not easily break. Good for different kinds of yarn – but a little difficult to handle for beginners as stitches move quickly when using these needles.

•Metal Needles

This type of needle is suitable for all yarn and wool types, and some experts also love using this kind of needle as they can maneuver the stitches quickly when using them; but it is advisable for novices to avoid this type as stitches tend to easily slip off the needle's tip.

For beginners, choosing the needle type that helps ease and improve learning is better. You can start off with bigger, easy-to-grip, non-slippery needles for a successful first attempt at knitting. Then, when you have the hang of it, you can try other kinds of needles to see if they would suit your preferences better.

Wools to Avoid

Beginner knitters have a lot to avoid when it comes to choosing wools or yarns. First off, you should be avoiding yarns that are very dark in color. As already mentioned, you may find great difficulty in seeing the stitches when using very dark-colored yarns. Start off with lighter colors, then move to darker ones when you have mastered the basics.

Yarns that have broken plies should also be avoided as you these will not result in a good-quality finished product. These types of yarns are very low quality. The best suggestion when you have purchased this kind of yarn is to return this to the store and get another.

Another characteristic of yarn that should be avoided are those types that easily split. Knitting yarn that easily splits is hard to work with and may cause your needle-top to go between the yarns. Using easily-split yarn may result in a product that is not to your liking.

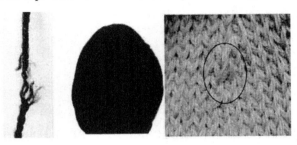

Other Knitting Equipment

After choosing the yarn and needle that you find suitable for your first knitting project, you still have to consider other equipment that is necessary for a successful project.

You should ensure that you have ready: scissors, tapes, darning needles and other supplies that might be of use. Buying extra pairs of needles (in case you lose or break any) and additional bundles of yarn is also essential to ensure that you have enough.

Chapter 2:
Learn How to Hold the Needle and Yarn

How to hold the needle and yarn in knitting depends on the person doing it. One person may feel more comfortable holding them one way, and another knitter in a different way. Another factor is which hand is dominant for the individual. Overall, you should just decide which way is more comfortable for you and just go with that.

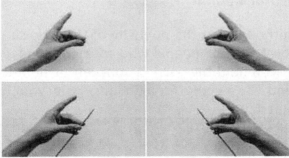

Easy way to hold a needle and yarn

Some may hold the yarn on their left hand, interlacing it between fingers and intertwining it on your pinky finger, and some may do it on the right side. Holding the needle in either hand is also possible, whichever is more comfortable for you – just make sure that you are holding onto it lightly and not gripping it.

Two types of knitting method

English Knitting Method

This method is best used by people who are more dominant in using their left hand. Placement of yarn in this method is in the non-dominant or right hand and the needle that is used in stitching is held by the dominant or left hand.

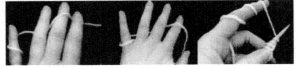

Continental Method

This method is just the opposite of the English practice and is best used by people who are right handed. In this method you hold the yarn in your left or non-dominant hand and the needle for stitching is in your right or dominant hand.

These are merely suggestions to make holding yarn and needles easier for beginners. You are not required to follow this exact position in holding your needle and yarn. As a beginner, you should also be able to experiment with what position is easier for you. Some people may even love to work with the stitching needle using their non-dominant hand. The decision is up to you. As long as you are comfortable and you find the position you choose easier, then there would be no adverse effects in the project's outcome.

How to make a simple pattern

•*Casting on*

Step one: Using your right hand hold your needle; and hold your yarn in your left hand.

Step two: Make a loose tie around your needle.

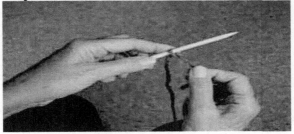

Step Three: Hold the needle with the loose tie of yarn in your left hand, and hold the other needle on you right. Then insert the needle on your right hand into the tie, making an X.

Step Four: Hold both needles in your left hand and hold the yarn in your right hand.

Step Five: loop the yarn you are holding in your right hand around the bottom needle in your left hand, and bring it in between the two needles.

Step Six: Bring the bottom needle out of the tie, pulling the yarn wrapped around it along.

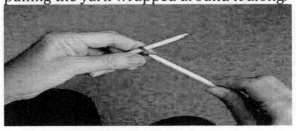

Step Seven: Now using the needle on your left

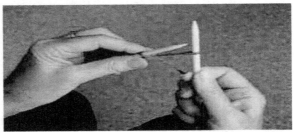

hand, insert it under the loop at the right needle and pull the right needle out.

Step eight: This would then give you two loops. Continue the same process until you get all the loops that you need.

You may do this the other way around if you are having difficulty using your right hand. Just follow the same steps and you will get the same results.

Chapter 3:
Basic Knitting Stitches for the Beginner

Common Knitting Stitches

•Stockinette Stitch

This is a commonly used knitting stitch for making sweaters and a lot of other knitting projects. This is created by knitting on the right side and purling on the wrong side, thus creating a "V" pattern.

Step one: the first step is: do a cast onto your needle, ensuring that you are using a flat needle.

Step two: Knit all the stitches that you need for the first row.

Step three: All the next row of stitching should be purled on the wrong side.

Step four: Just repeat the process until you have reached the desired length.

•Garter Stitch

This kind of stitch results in a reversible, flat and ridged fabric that does not roll. It is also the most fundamental of all stitch patterns and is easily done by knitting every row.

Step one: Start doing your cast on stitches onto your needle.

Step two: Bring your two needles into position.

Step three: Bring the needle on your right hand into the first loop of yarn that you are holding on your left hand.

Step four: Wrap the yarn around the back of the right needle and in between the two needles.

Step five: Pull back the right needle using your hand, making sure to bring along the yarn that you have looped around it.

Step six: Pull the loop off the left needle. This can be done by pulling the right needle carefully, to get the old loop from the left needle.

Step seven: All the cast on stitches should be knit the same way until you have no more of those stitches on your left needle.

Step eight: Switch the needles between your left and right hand side. Then start knitting your second row in exactly the same way.

•Rib Stitch

This stitch is done by working alternating purls and knits, which then creates a vertical striped effect. This stitch results in having the "V" column, seen on the stockinette stitch, on its every other column.

Step 1:

•Seed Stitch

These stitches are a combination of knit 1 and purl 1 and are known to be the opposite of rib stitch. In making this you, have to work using the reverse principles of stockinette stitch, and knit the knit and purl the purls.

Knit and Purl

This may seem to confuse a lot of beginners, especially when you are only given the instruction of a knit and a purl to make a pattern. A knit and a purl is basically just the opposite of each other: a knit on the front is a purl on the back side.

Knit

Step 1: Insert your right needle into the right or inside part of the first stitch on the left needle.

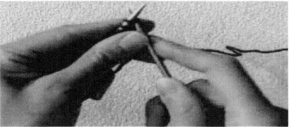

Step 2: Make an X with both needles.

Step 3: Using your left hand, hold both needles.

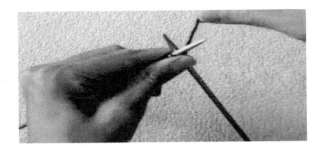

Step 4: Then wrap your working yarn around your right needle, bringing it in between the two needles

Step 5: Pull back your right needle, making sure to bring along the wrapped yarn.

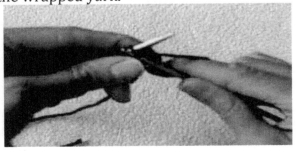

Step 6: Then slip the first stitch off the left needle and onto your right. There you have your first stitch.

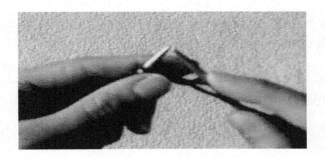

Purl is just the exact opposite of knit: the difference is that the right needle would be inserted through the front of the stitch and the working yarn will be wrapped coming from the front. Everything else will be just doing the same pattern.

Rib or Ribbing

This basically notates the number of knits and purls in the project. This type of stitching also shows a pattern of vertical line made with stockinette stitch, followed by another vertical line made by using the reverse stockinette stitch. There are also two types of rib or ribbing in knitting

- 1 x 1 Ribbing
  A project that has 1 knit followed by 1 purl is already considered as 1 x 1 ribbing

- 2 x 2 Ribbing
  Stitching 2 knits that is then followed by 2 purls

Eyelet and Lace

Step 1: Knit the lace by starting from the left and place the lace to the back of the work.

Step 2: Insert the needle into the first stitch and through the first eyelet hole in the lace.

Step 3: Loop yarn over the needle and complete the stitch.

Step 4: Keep the tension loose and repeat the same procedure to the end of the row; then cut the lace.

Cable and twist

This stitch pattern gives a very beautiful cable twisting design to your knitted projects. This is also very simple to do. Just follow these very simple steps:

Step 1: In these examples, the knitter is using a 3 x 3

cable twist stitch. This was done purling the first three stitches.

Step 2: You then need to first separate the next three stitches as you are not going to use them yet. You can use another needle to separate these stitches.

Step 3: Knit the next three stitches that are on the left-hand needle.

Step 4: After that you can now bring in the needle with the three stitches that you separated earlier. Now you can knit those 3 stitches as well.

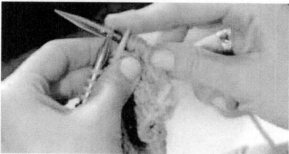

You would then be able to see the cable twist pattern or effect that this makes, as seen on the picture beside.

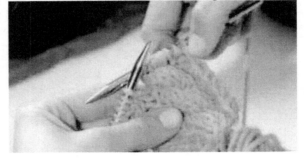

Chapter 4:
Learn to Knit a Seed Stitch

First, basic seed stitch: step by step instructions.

How to put seed stitch together. Step by step instructions. Uses of seed stitches.

Step 1: First you need to cast on the amount of stitches the pattern calls for. As you can see in this photo above, we have cast on 10 stitches.

Step 2: Now we begin our seed stitch pattern pretty much the same as: one pearl, one knit. Always remember: knitting the first stitch, purling the next. So that is what we are going to do right here.

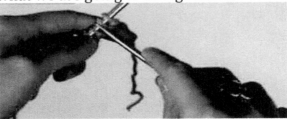

Step 3: Just knit and purl the entire way across, going to the left side, and just make sure you alternate your stitches.

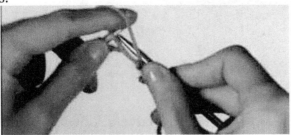

Step 4: Now you are going to flip your work. You remember the one knit one purl ribbing, but right now you need to find what is on the first row. You need to check it before you proceed. As you can see on the right side, it's a knit followed by the purl, a knit and then a purl. For the knit one and the purl one, you knit the knits and purl the purls, but for the seed stitch we need to completely alternate it.

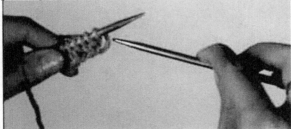

Step 5: This is very important for the seed stitch: anytime you see a knit stitch, you need to purl; and every time you see a bump/purl, we're going to knit into the next stitch.

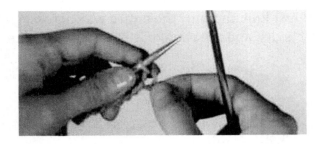

Step 6: So right now we have a knit stitch in the row below, so we need to bring the yarn in the front and we're going to purl it. After that, we have a bump/purl: it means we're going to knit the stitch above it and then we're just going to alternate the entire way across. Remember, we're just knitting your purls and purling into your knits. It's very simple; you do not need to follow a pattern at all.

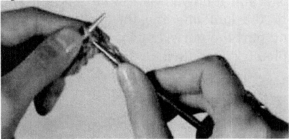

Step 7: Now you can already see some kind of shaping, with bumps and dips.

Step 8: Now we'll look at the row below and you can see we begin with a bump and after that we have a knit, which means we have to knit the stitch and purl into the stitch. So again, knit into your purls and purls into your knits and then alternate the entire way across your row. This also works if you're knitting in a round. If you use this method and all you do is just pay attention on the row below, you don't need to follow a pattern.

Step 9. Now you can see the finish and how a seed stitch looks. It's a very simple and pretty stitch.

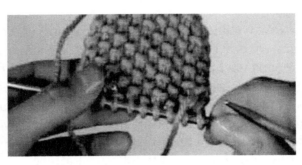

Putting the Seed Stitch together

Step 1: First thing you do is a cast on, and you can do this by first creating a slipknot. Make a loop out of your yarn

Step 2: Pull the yarn from the front of your two fingers and then there is your very own slipknot.

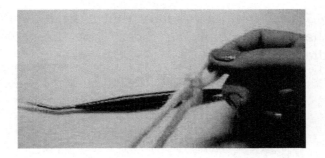

Step 3: Put your needle inside the loop or slipknot that you have made and tighten it to avoid slipping.

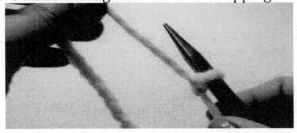

Step 4: You should then be ready to start casting on. Just follow the same steps as seen in Chapter 1.

Step 5: Cast on until you have your desired number of stitches. (This sample has been done using circular needles).

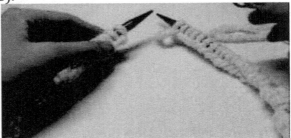

Step 6: You may also use a marker when doing this to ensure that you are able to recognize the edge of the row.

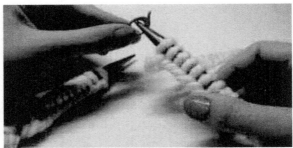

Step 7: After placing the marker, you can now start knitting.

Step 8: For the first row, you have to remember that you have to knit one and then purl.

Step 9: Continue this pattern until you have reached the end of the row. Then move your marker from the left needle to the right needle again.

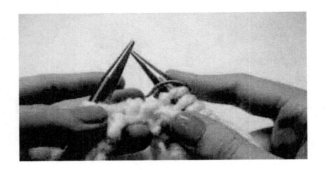

Step 10: After placing the marker on the right needle, you can now start to knit, but using the pattern in reverse. This is to purl one and then knit one.

Step 11: Continue doing so, making sure to K1 and P1, then P1 and K1, in alternate rows, until you reach the desired length of your project.

Joining the Seed Stitch:

Step 1: When you have achieved the desired length of your project, you remove the marker as you do not need it anymore.

Step 2: Now you start binding off. You can do this by first doing a knit one and a purl one.

Step 3: After doing one knit and one purl, you are able to see the first two stitches on your right needle.

Step 4: Gently slip your left needle into the second loop in your right needle, as seen in the picture.

Step 5: Using your left needle, you have to then slip the second loop over the first loop.

Step 6: Repeat the process, until you reach the end of the row.

Step 7: At the end of the row, you can see these remaining two yarns.

Step 8: Using your left hand, hold the part where the two yarns meet and pull the extra yarn to tighten it. Then cut the remaining yarn.

Just follow these simple steps and you will be able to stitch using the seed stitch pattern and bind or join them like a pro in no time.

All you need is a little patience, a little focus and you will inevitably end up loving this new hobby.

Uses of seed stitch

Seed stitch is a very commonly used pattern of stitch in clothing, kitchenware, furniture and also in fashion. This is not only because of its unique design in stitching but the durability of its finished product. Seed stitch pattern creates a bumpy surface and does not curl easily. Seed stitch also creates a stretchy texture when finished – making it particularly suitable for knitted clothes or other items that may benefit from a slight yield in the fabric.

You can make different kinds of clothes, like scarves, hats, sweaters and socks. You can also make a lot of kitchen accessories with this type of stitch, such as placemats, pot-holders and coasters. Furniture-wise, you can make seat covers, rugs, a placemat for your expensive vase, and some even pillowcases. For fashion accessories, you can make different types of bags, cellphone covers, or even a coin purse with a striking, art pattern stitch.

Chapter 5:
Add Stitches of Interest

Once you have gained a firm grasp of the basic stitches in knitting, you can start experimenting more – not only in trying complicated patterns, but also creating your own stitch patterns.

The most important thing to remember when starting your very own project using a new stitch is to always remember the pattern that you are using for the stitch. Beginners can easily loose track of the pattern when knitting ones which are complicated.

Before starting any project, you should also make sure to make a gauge swatch. A gauge swatch will be able to show you how many loops you should cast on so to get the desired size of article. You do not want a finished product that is smaller or larger than the size you would like.

The Linen stitch

Knitting the Linen Stitch

This stitch is also known as the fabric stitch, and is one of those patterns that are able to achieve different looks just by changing the color scheme of your knitting. It also creates a beautiful woven effect that does not curl due to the type of stitch used, which is the slip stitch.

Linen stitch pattern

This should be worked over an even number of stitches and do Slip stitches purl wise.

Row 1: *Knit 1, slip 1 with yarn in front; Repeat from * to end. Turn.

Row 2: *Purl 1, slip 1 with yarn in back; Repeat from * to end. Turn.

Solid Color Linen Stitch

In doing this knitting, you have to work every row in the same color. This will then result in a beautifully textured solid fabric. As seen on photo below, the wrong side of the knitting looks like a seed stitch which makes it reversible. This stitch can be used in a variety of projects like placemats and scarfs.

Two-color Linen Stitch

The two color pattern is done by using two colors and alternating them every two rows. You have to work with the first color for two rows then the second color for two rows. This two color pattern enhances the woven effect and has a very gorgeous pattern.

Three-color Linen Stitch

Adding a third color to your linen stitch will result in having a cool looking speckled fabric. In doing this pattern you have to work on your first row using your first color then switch to your second color on the second row and the third one on the third row. Continue doing this each row using the same colors and you will have a very beautiful three-color speckled fabric.

Row 1: Color 1

Row 2: Color 2

Row 1: Color 3

Row 2: Color 1

Row 1: Color 2

Row 2: Color 3

Working in the round

When you are working in the round, the right side of the fabric is always facing you. As a result, you will have to change the pattern up a bit.

Linen stitch in the round

this should be worked over an even number of stitches.

Round 1: *K 1, slip 1 with yarn in front; Repeat from * around.

Round 2: *Slip 1 with yarn in front, K 1; Repeat from * around.

The Linen stitch can be used in a variety of patterns and projects. You may even find yourself easily loving this stitch in knitting. I would highly suggest doing solids first and then proceed to two or three colored when you have mastered doing the stitch.

Tips on Knit without Looking

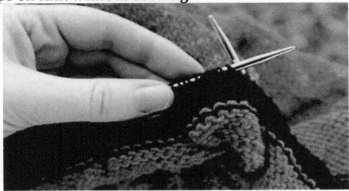

Many knitters that have mastered this craft can already knit without looking at their yarn and needles due to expert's knowledge and familiarity with the handled material. Many people who have not mastered this yet have also tried and wanted to have this skill in knitting. Here are some tips to help you learn this skill as well and maybe start to knit without looking.

Tip #1: Use your left hand or stitch markers for guidance.

When trying to knit without looking at you yarn stitches and needles. There would be the time that you would miss doing some of the stitches. This would make thing more difficult for you for you would then have to do your knitting over which then takes a lot more time.

To avoid this kind of problem, you can use your left-hand fingers to feel the stitches that are coming up. Another tip is to also use stitch markers to be able to know if you have reached the end of your cast on and to make sure that you are aware if something difficult is coming on.

Steps to using DIY Rainbow Knitting Stitch Markers

Stitch Markers are very important tools in knitting especially for beginners which can be easily confused with the number of stitches and an entire row. Using them will aid you in knowing that you have reached the end of a row and will greatly assist you in changing the type of stitch you are then using for you'll know that you have reached the next row.

Materials:

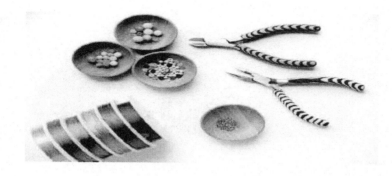

- •Assorted beads
- •Tiger Tail Wire
- •Crimp Beads
- •Wire cutter pliers
- •Flat nosed pliers

You can decide whatever bead combination would fit your taste as long as you would keep it to about 1 cm to ½ inch. This is to avoid too much weight and dangle when using the stitch marker.

Crimp beads may also be used to help lock other beads in place.

Tiger tail wire is made up of strands of very fine steel which are twisted together. These are coated with plastic or nylon, which creates a tough and resilient beading wire. You can get them in silver and other assorted colors. It holds its shape when bent so it won't get tangled in your knitting.

Making the Stitch Marker

Step 1: Cut about 3" of tiger tail wire off the roll.

Step 2: Gently fold it in half (don't crease the top) and thread beads onto both wires ends in this order: crimp bead, decorative beads, and crimp bead.

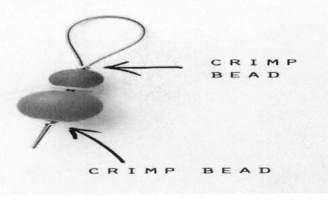

CRIMP BEAD

CRIMP BEAD

Step 3: Adjust the loop to your desired size and firmly pinch the top and bottom beads with flat nose pliers. Make sure the crimp beads are butted up against the decorative beads to stop them sliding about.

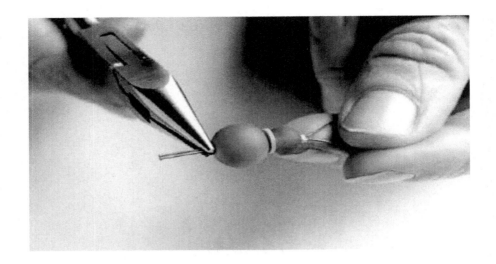

This is what the crimp beads look like when that are squished.

Step 4: Cut the excess wire as close to the crimp bead as possible to avoid snagging on knitting.

Now you are ready to use your very own DIY Rainbow Stitch Markers. Not only will this aid you in knitting, but they are also very fun to look at.

Examples of what the end result of knitting with markers looks like

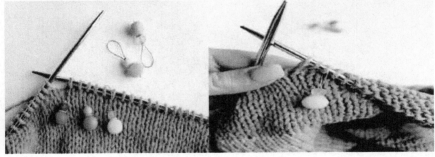

Tip #2: Learn how to fix a mistake

You are very prone to making mistakes especially when you are not looking. It will also be very time consuming to do the entire row or rows that you have done. The best solution to this is to learn how to fix mistakes like picking a drop stitch; correcting errors in ribbing and etc. this can be easily learned by searching for best techniques online. Examples of mistakes and stitch to correct error below.

Fixing Knitting Mistakes

Mistakes are commonly made in knitting, not only for beginners but also for those who are already experts in this skill. The only difference between beginners and experts is that experts have also mastered the skill of fixing knitting mistakes. But it does not mean that beginners do not have the ability to do this also. It might just take a little patience and practice and you'll be able to fix knitting mistakes like a pro in no time.

Spotting a Knitting Mistake

In spotting a mistake in your knitting project, the first thing you have to do is see clearly where the mistake was made. This can be done by placing your knitting on any flat surface. Then count the numbers of stitches on your knitting, if it is the right number, then you have not dropped any stitch. If everything is good with the number of stitches, you have to then look at your knitting for anything that does not look right. Be careful in handling your knitting, make sure that you do not pull, push or agitate any of the stitches.

Tinking

This method of fixing a knitting mistake can only be used if the mistake is made of the current or previous row. The right thing about this approach is that you do not have to rip everything. Instead, you just tink back.

Step 1:

The first step is inserting your left needle from the front part to back then into the stitch that is right below the first stitch on your right needle.

Step 2:

The first stitch should be slipped off the right needle.

Step 3:

Unravel the yarn.

Repeat steps 1-3 till you come to the stitch that is before the one where you made a mistake. Then continue knitting.

Frogging

Frogging is a knitting method that is done if the mistake made was done several rows ago. This got its name by actually what you are doing with this method which is to "rip it, rip it, rip it" almost like the sound of a frog.

Step 1:

Keep your work on a flat surface and carefully take your needles from your work leaving stitches open.

Step 2:

Pull the yarn to undo the stitches. When reaching the row that is above the row where the mistake was made, pull the yarn carefully to keep your stitches even.

Step 3:

Pick up stitches by using one of the needles. If you are using your right needle, you have to then insert your needle into each stitch from back to front. If you pick up stitches using your left needle, insert your needle into each stitch from front to back. Make sure that you have not dropped any stitch and the number of stitches are the same number as when you were starting to knit.

Life Line

Making a lifeline is an excellent idea when you are doing difficult patterns. Especially if you have noticed that you are prone to doing a lot of tinking and frogging when knitting.

Step 1:

Thread a piece of scrap yarn into a wool needle. The length of the scrap yarn should be about twice the width of your project.

Step 2:

Keeping stitches on your knitting needle snake the wool needle with scrap yarn through every stitch of your project.

Step 3:

Make a knot or a bow at each end of the scrap yarn to keep it from slipping.

Frogging if a mistake would be faster and easier with a lifeline. You just have to rip them all the way to where you have your lifeline made. Slipping your needle into the stitches would also be easier if a life line is present and you would be sure not to miss any stitches.

Tip #3: Warm-up

Prior to starting your knitting without looking, you have to first look and examine carefully how your hands are working with the material. By doing this, you would have increased familiarization and improve success in knitting without looking

Tip #4: Put intervals between looking and not

Especially for beginners, you must always keep in mind that it is acceptable to look. Learning is not an instant process and doing intervals will greatly help you assess your capabilities and easily correct any mistakes done when not looking. This will also be excellent practice for those who are just starting to master this skill.

Tip #5: Use the right pattern

When starting to knit without looking you should begin by doing fundamental and repetitive stitches. This would me much easier especially for those who are still mastering this skill. Avoid using complicated patterns for this will only cause frustration and mistakes.

Chapter 6:
Using Different Stitches to their Best Advantage

Getting accustomed to knitting

Learning would not be fully felt and gained if you were unable to practice and perfect the craft. Another tip that beginners should know is that they should first master the basics before moving on to more complicated stitches.

In learning the basic stitches first, you are able to develop your rhythm, speed and know how to hold the needle and yarn with ease without gripping them too much – all of which will aid you in lengthening focus, patience and your love for the craft.

Moving to complicated stitches immediately may cause exasperation, tiredness and loss of curiosity. It is also usually the reason why some people do not continue with this hobby, for they lose interest in this form of art due to these factors.

Knitting tips for Beginners

•Use inexpensive yarns at first

Being a beginner, your first few knitting projects will probably be a few trials. Going for cheap yarns at first will save you money. Practicing this craft is essential so that you become a good knitter. You can still practice effectively using cheaper yarns, and then move to more expensive and exclusive ones when you know that you are ready.

•Use basic yarns at first

Going to your local yarn store, you might see different kinds and colors of yarn that tempt you. Hold off for a little bit until you are capable of doing the basic stitches with ease. Going for basics first will aid you in learning – as some specialty yarns are very hard to handle.

•Relax

When you are starting to knit, you should bear in mind that your hands may get tired. Stop and relax when you feel that you can no longer knit. This is not a marathon; you can always learn at your own pace and in your own time.

•Be inspired

Nothing can beat a person who is inspired in doing something – that is the force that would keep you going no matter what you encounter in this new learning experience. You may be able to get inspiration from seeing very lovely knitted articles, or wanting to create something special for someone you love or even for yourself. Whatever the reason is, as long as you are inspired to do something then it will bring you great happiness.

Creating a Sampler

Being a beginner, it would also be better to try knitting using the basic stitches first. Before you start on your first big project, it would also be better if you are able to try these different stitches and make a sampler from each kind of stitch.

Steps in Creating a Sampler:

Step 1: Pick the type of stitch or pattern that you want to try first.

Step 2: For beginners, choosing yarns that are thicker is better as they are easier to handle and maneuver.

Step 3: Pick a needle that is of the appropriate size or gauge as your yarn. Also choose needles that are smooth but do not let yarn slip easily.

Step 4: Start making your sampler.

Convenient Sampler Size for Beginners

Samplers can range from 4 x 4 to 8 x 8 square. Just do something that you would be more comfortable with. By making samplers, you are able to see what the actual stitches would look like in your project. Get ideas about which ones you prefer to use now and which would be better for future projects. These samplers are not be a total waste of time, attention and money as they can be used to make great pot holders, coasters, etcetera.

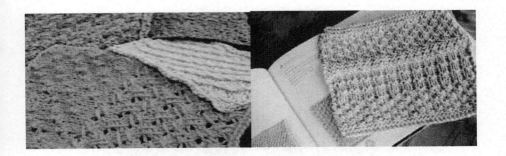

"Increases" and "Decreases" in Knitting

These are terms that are commonly used in knitting. They primarily denote how the knitter adjusts the number of stitches in a row to increase or decrease, in order to make the parts of an item they are knitting into the appropriate size.

Increase Stitches

This means you are adding an extra stitch (or loop) to your needle. This will increase the length of the row by 1 stitch, thus increasing the width.

Decrease Stitches

This is when you are removing a stitch (or loop) from your needle. This will shrink the length of the row by 1 stitch, thus decreasing the width.

Increase Stitches

Basically, you are knitting two stitches like normal, but the first time you knit a stitch you do not slip the stitch off the left needle.

Step 1: Knit a stitch, but don't slip the stitch off your left needle

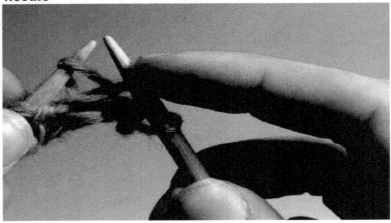

Step 2: Instead, bring your right needle through the top stitch on your left needle, and knit another stitch.

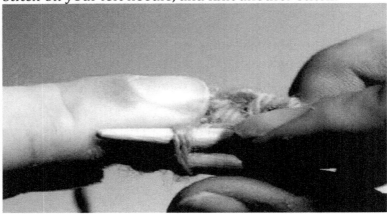

Step 3: Now remove the stitch from the left needle

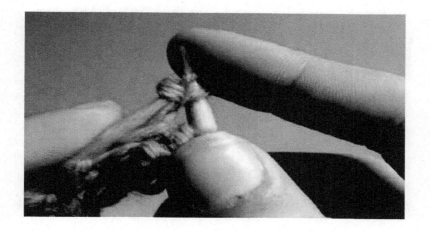

This would then be how it would look like on your right hand needle. You have made 2 stitches from 1 stitch.

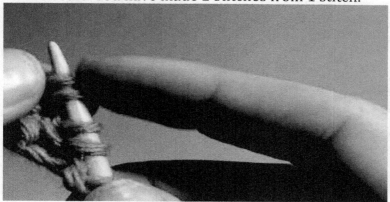

Increase: Yarn Over: This technique leaves holes in yarn. It is usually done with decorative stitches. When you want to leave an eyelet in your yarn use this method

Step 1: Knit a Stitch

Step 2: Wrap yarn once around the right needle to make an extra loop on right needle.

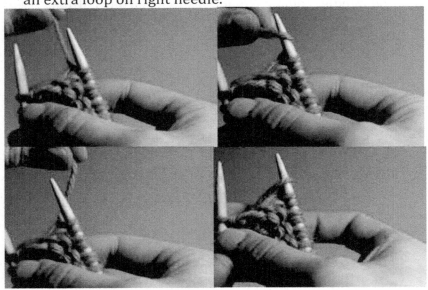

Step 3: Continue Knitting

Decrease Stitches; Knitting Two Together: everything is the same as making a knit stitch, but instead of passing the needle through the top stitch on the left needle, pass the needle through the top two stitches and knit as if it were one stitch.

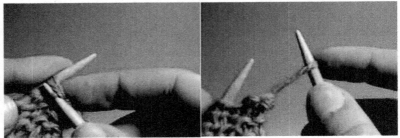

Decrease: KRPR

KRPR = Knit, Return Pass, Return

Decrease: A decrease stitch usually looks like one stitch is overlapping another. Decreasing stitches can also be made from the left or from the right. Here is the step by step instruction on how to do a decreasing stitch.

Step 1: Knit one stitch

Step 2: Return stitch you just knitted back onto the left needle

Step 3: Take the second stitch on left needle using your right needle and **pass** it over the top stitch on the left needle and off the needle

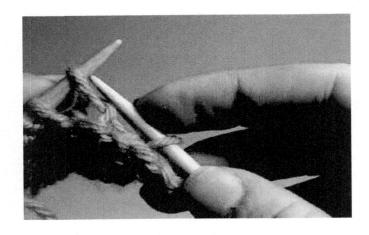

Step 4: Return the stitch on the left needle back to right needle.

Left Slanting Decrease

Step 1: Slip two stitches from left needle onto right needle

Step 2: Pass left needle back through two stitches you just slipped onto the right needle. Making sure to keep the stitches on the right needle.

Step 3: Knit a stitch by wrapping the yarn around the tip of the right needle and pulling the right needle through the stitches.

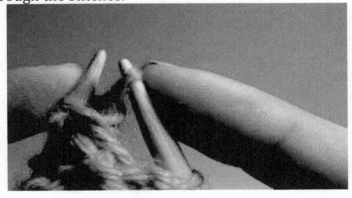

Step 4: Slip the two stitches that you have knitted off the left needle. You have now knitted one stitch out of two stitches onto your right needle.

This skills or method in knitting will aid you in creating many beautiful patterns ranging from different shapes. All you need is a little patience and practice and you will sure master this in no time.

Scalloped Knitting Edge Stitch:

This type of knitting edge pattern offers an exquisite effect to your knitting project. It is also quite easy to do once you have mastered it, but if you are a beginner then just follow this few simple steps.

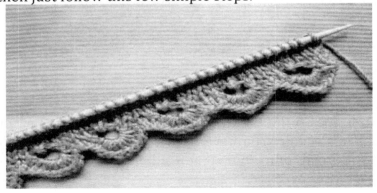

Step 1: First you have to cast on your stitches (a multiple of 11 + 2). You can do a 1 needle cast on. Purl 1 row.

Step 2: Knit the first 2 stitches for the selvedge, and then knit 1.

Step 3: Slip the last stitch that you have knit back to the left needle.

Step 4: Then, you have to lift the next 8 stitches over the stitch you just moved.

It will look like this. You'll have the best looking scallops when you pull up the yarn tightly on the stitch where the other 8 are all looped over.

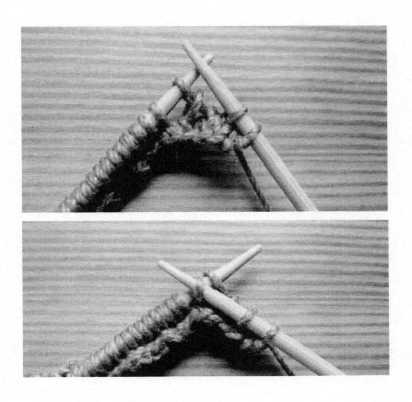

Step 5: Yarn over twice.

Step 6: Knit 2 to finish the loop, then knit 1 to start the next repeat.

Step 7: You have to then Slip it to the left needle and continue the repeat until the end of the row.

Step 8: After you've finished the entire row, turn it around and knit 1, then purl 2 together. If you've never done that before it's exactly what it sounds like. Work it like any other purl stitch, but with 2 stitches together instead of 1.

Step 9: Drop one of the yarn overs off the needle.

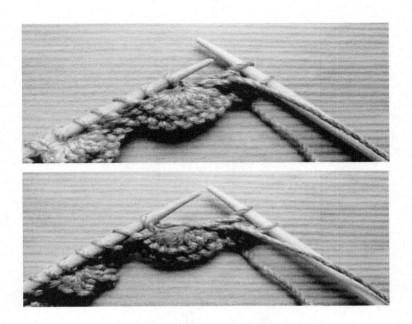

Step 10: Now you have to turn the big loop around. Pass it on the right by placing the right needle into the back of the loop as shown on photo below.

Step 11: Then pass it back to the left.

Step 12: Knit the stitch like how you usually do, but don't pull it off the left needle.

Step 13: Knit into the back of the loop and pull it off the needle.

Step 14: Pick the loop back up with the left needle as shown. Knit into the front and back of the stitch again.

All that turning, dropping, and picking up may seem a bit silly, but it will really result in a beautiful knitting project.

Step 15: Purl 1 stitch and then start the repeat over with the purl 2 together. At the end of the row, you'll knit 1 selvedge stitch.

You can also add a few rows of stockinette stitch to show the finished effect better. If you wanted your scallops tighter you could use 1 yarn over instead of 2, but it's probably important to test that to be sure it won't pull on whatever you knit above it.

The back side of the scallop is also as pretty as the front side, thus making it very much reversible.

Tutorial Pattern for Beginners

Knitting patterns can sometimes be bought along with the yarn and other supplies. This would be easier for beginners, to avoid wrong yarn and needle choice. But if you are someone that does not want to try very easy, ready-to-knit patterns with supplies, you can search online for free patterns. There are a lot of downloadable patterns available, especially from big yarn manufacturers' websites and other knitting sites.

Knitting a Beanie with Straight Needles

This is perfect for beginners who find it easier to use straight knitting needles.

Materials:

- •Measuring tape
- •200 yards worsted weight yarn
- •Knitting needles

•Scissors

•Tapestry needle

Starting the Project

Step 1: Make a gauge, which can be done by knitting a small swatch. Cast on at least 2 inches worth of yarn. Knit a few rows and then use your measuring tape to count the number of stitches in one inch.

Step 2: Cast on the number of stitches needed by using your gauge. This can be done by first measuring the circumference of the wearer's head, or you can approximate. For example, to knit a hat with a 15-inch circumference, with a gauge of 4 stitches in one inch, you should cast on 60 stitches.

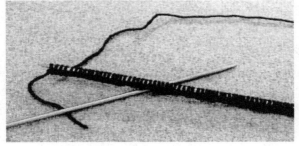

Step 3: Start by knitting 10 rows in garter stitch.

Working the Hat

Step 1: Change to stockinette stitch, and alternate knit rows and purl rows. Continue until the hat measures 6 inches from the cast-on edge. This is a good length for a child's hat. For an adult hat, keep knitting for another 2 inches, ending with a purl row.

Step 2: Knit eight stitches and then knit two stitches together. Repeat from across the row. When you no longer have enough stitches left on the needle to achieve this, simply knit to the last two stitches, and knit two together. Purl one row.

Step 3: Knit seven stitches and then knit two stitches together. Repeat from across the row. When you no longer have enough stitches left on the needle to achieve this, knit to the last two stitches, and knit two together. Purl one row. Repeat this process, decreasing the number of knit stitches by one, until, at last, you knit one, and then knit two stitches together.

Finishing the Hat

Step 1: Cut the yarn, leaving a long tail – at least 20 inches. Thread the tail into the tapestry needle and insert the tapestry needle into the remaining stitches, lifting them off the knitting needle. Pull the yarn tight to close the hole.

Step 2: Hold the edges of the hat together, seam the sides of the hat closed. This can be done by stitching one side to the next with the tapestry needle. Insert the needle into the same row on each side of the hat.

Step 3: When you reach the bottom of the hat, turn it inside out. Weave the yarn into the wrong side of the hat for a couple of inches to hide the tail. Cut the yarn close to the fabric.

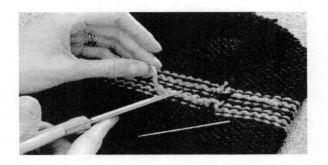

Knitting Golf Head Covers

This would be a great gift idea if your special someone is into golfing. This makes this gift a very thoughtful one and they would be able to use it in doing one of their most enjoyed hobbies.

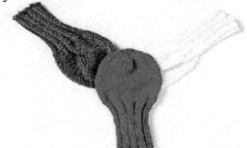

Knitting the Sock

Step 1: Cast 54 stitches onto the smaller needles, distributing evenly among three of the four needles.

Step 2: Join stitches without twisting.

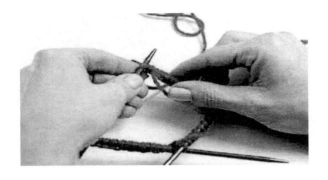

Step 3: Knit 3 stitches and purl 3 stitches all the way around.

Step 4: Repeat step 3 until the piece measures approximately 5 inches from the cast-on edge.

Knitting the Head

Step 1: Change to larger needles.

Step 2: Work in stockinette stitch by knitting every stitch all the way around until the piece measures approximately 11 1/2 inches from the cast-on edge.

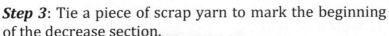

Step 3: Tie a piece of scrap yarn to mark the beginning of the decrease section.

Decreasing

Step 1: Knit 1 stitch and then knit 2 stitches together. Repeat this pattern all the way around.

Step 2: Knit every stitch all the way around.

Step 3: Repeat steps 1 and 2 twice more. You will have 16 stitches remaining.

Step 4: After that, knit 2 stitches together all the way around. You will have 8 stitches remaining.

Step 5: Cut yarn, leaving a 6 inch tail. Thread the tail through the yarn needle and through remaining stitches. Pull tight to close. Weave in loose ends.

Baby Headband

Material

- 100 yards worsted weight yarn

- US 7 12-inch circular needles
- 20 inches of 1/2 inch-wide elastic
- Tape measure
- Scissors
- Needle and thread
- Yarn needle
- Stitch marker

Step 1: This headband requires only about 100 yards of yarn, so it's a good project for using up scraps. Worsted weight works best because it's thick enough to hide the elastic underneath. Please see the last slide for an itemized list of tools and materials.

Step 2: Cast on 68 stitches and place marker. Knit for 1 inch. Purl 1 row. Knit for 1 inch. Cut yarn, leaving a 30-inch tail.

Step 3: Cut a piece of elastic 15 inches long. Overlap by 1 inch and sew around the edge of the overlap with needle and thread.

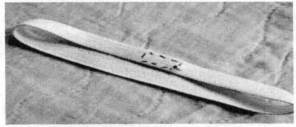

Step 4: Use your yarn needle and the long tail of yarn attached to your knitting; hem the elastic into the headband by inserting the yarn needle through the first stitch on your knitting needle. Place the elastic directly behind your knitting, then reach around the elastic to insert your yarn needle through the first stitch at the cast-on edge. You will have sewn a loop around the elastic.

Step 5: Insert your yarn needle through the next stitch on your knitting needle, reach around the elastic again, and insert your yarn needle into the next stitch at the cast-on edge. Repeat until all stitches are sewn together. Cut yarn and weave in ends using your yarn needle, being careful not to pull too tightly – the headband must have some room to stretch.

Step 6: Cast on 40 stitches to make your flower. Knit 1 row. *K1, cast off 7 stitches, repeat from* to the end of your needle.

Step 7: Cut yarn, leaving a 12-inch tail. Thread your yarn needle, and insert it through the remaining stitches on your knitting needles. Pull tight to make a flower. Leave tail on flower.

Step 8: Block the flower by rinsing it in cool water for five minutes, reshaping it, and laying it flat to dry.

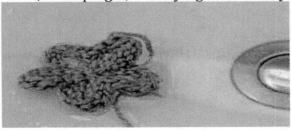

Step 9: Using the tail of the flower, sew it onto the headband.

Beard Heat

Materials

- Large knitting needles
- Yarn (any color)
- Large sewing needle

Mustache

Step 1: Begin with the mustache part of the hat. Cast one stitch; then knit front and back to make two stitches. Knit one row. Add two more stitches to the next row. Knit one row. Add two more stitches (6 total). Knit three rows.

Step 2: To decrease rows, knit 2 together, knit, knit 2 together (should have 4 stitches). Knit one row. Repeat first decrease row (should have 2 stitches). Knit one row.

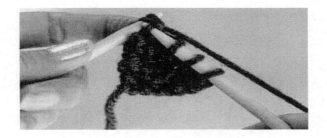

Step 3: Add 2 stitches (repeat Step 1) to start the second part of the mustache.

Step 4: Decrease rows by repeating Step 2.

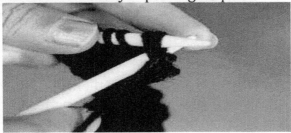

Step 5: Cast off (you should have two stitches left after Step 2).

Beard

Step 1: Cast on six stitches. Knit six rows. Knit three stitches then knit front and back to add two more stitches. Knit one row. Add two more stitches. Knit one row. Continue this pattern until you have 20 stitches. Knit three rows.

Step 2: Knit 5 stitches, knit 2 together twice to decrease stitches. Knit one row. Continue this pattern until you have decreased to 6 stitches. Knit one row.

Step 3: Cast off.

Step 4: Using a large sewing needle, sew the separate beard and mustache pieces together at each end of the mustache.

Slippers

If you're a beginner, the idea of knitting something in the round may be intimidating. You don't have to master the art of double-pointed needles in order to make knit slippers for beginners. You can knit slippers for beginners on two straight needles and seam them together when you finish. A basic pattern can work for any yarn style or foot size, if you simply add or subtract stitches from your initial cast-on.

Things You'll Need

- Yarn
- Knitting needles
- Large-eye blunt needle

Step 1: Cast on enough stitches to make a width of approximately 15 inches for a child's slipper; for an adult, cast on enough to make 16 to 18 inches. Knit every row until the piece measures 4 inches high (5 to 5 1/2 inches for adults).

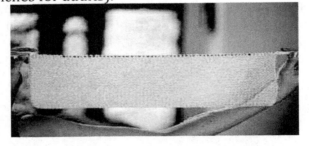

Step 2: Cast off the first 2, 3 or 4 inches' worth of stitches (for child, adult small and adult large) at the beginning of the next row and then knit across the row. Cast off the same number of stitches at the beginning of the subsequent row and then knit across. On the third

decrease row, cast off half as many stitches at the beginning of the row and knit across; repeat this on the fourth decrease row.

Step 3: Knit every row for 2, 3 or 4 more inches. On the next row, knit two stitches together all the way across the row. Knit the next row evenly. Knit two stitches together across the following row.

Step 4: Cut your working yarn, leaving an 18-inch tail. Thread this tail onto a large-eye blunt needle and slide it through each stitch loop left on the needle, removing them from the knitting needle as you go. Pull tightly to cinch the toe portion of the slipper closed.

Step 5: Stitch back and forth in a shoelace or looping pattern up the toe and top of the slipper to close the side seams together on top of the slipper. Continue stitching until the seam is long enough to cover the top of the wearer's foot. Knot the yarn and weave in the ends.

Step 6: Close the seam that will go from the back of the heel to the back of the ankle. To do this, thread another length of yarn on a large-eye blunt needle and use it to stitch this seam together as previously. Fold down the front edges of the ankle portion of the slipper into points like a collar.

There are still a lot more patterns to choose from. All you have to do search online and you will be bombarded by the tremendous number of patterns available for use. As, a beginner, it is highly advisable to try and start with those that are easy to knit. Then when you are highly capable, you can start experimenting and do more difficult patterns

Made in the USA
Coppell, TX
17 October 2021